A Primary Source History of

SLAVERY IN THE UNITED STATES

by Allison Crotzer Kimmel

Consultant:
Cassandra L. Newby-Alexander, PhD
Professor of History
Director, Joseph Jenkins Roberts Center
for African Diaspora Studies
Norfolk State University
Norfolk, Virginia

CAPSTONE PRESS
a capstone imprint

DETROIT PUBLISHING

Fact Finders are published by Capstone Press,
1710 Roe Crest Drive, North Mankato, Minnesota 56003.
www.capstonepub.com

Library of Congress Cataloging-in-Publication Data
Kimmel, Allison Crotzer.
A primary source history of slavery in the United States / by Allison Crotzer Kimmel.
pages cm. — (Fact finders. Primary source history)
Summary: "Uses primary sources to tell the story of slavery in the United States"— Provided by publisher.
Includes bibliographical references and index.
ISBN 978-1-4914-1839-0 (library binding) — ISBN 978-1-4914-1843-7 (pbk.) — ISBN 978-1-4914-1847-5 (ebook pdf)
1. Slavery—United States—History—Juvenile literature. 2. African Americans—History—To 1863—Juvenile literature. I. Title.
E441.K586 2015
306.3′620973—dc23   2014020438

Editorial Credits
Jennifer Besel, editor; Kyle Grenz, designer; Wanda Winch, media researcher;
    Kathy McColley, production specialist

Photo Credits
Capstone, 19, 21 (bottom); Chicago Historical Museum, 23; clipart.com, 6; Corbis, 9 (top), Bettmann, cover (b), National Geographic Society, 18; Courtesy of Archives and Special Collections, Dickinson College, Carlisle, PA, 14; CriaImages.com: Jay Robert Nash Collection, 17; Getty Images: Hulton Archive, 15; Library of Congress: Broadsides, leaflets, and pamphlets from America and Europe/ Printed Ephemera Collection, cover (top), 12, Prints and Photographs Division, 1 (all), 5, 24, 27, Rare Books and Special Collections Division, 22; National Archives and Records Administration, 21 (t), ourdocuments.gov, 25, 29; North Wind Pictures and Archives, 13; Photographs and Print Division, Schomburg Center for Research in Black Culture, The New York Public Library, Astor, Lenox and Tilden Foundations, 16; Thinkstock: Stockbyte, 10; William L. Clements Library, University of Michigan, 9 (b)

The author dedicates this book to her brother Andrew, a fellow history buff.

Printed in Canada
092014   008478FRS15

TABLE OF CONTENTS

COLONIAL SLAVE TRADE 4

SLAVERY IN A NEW NATION 8

LIFE AS A SLAVE 12

A DIVIDED NATION 20

FREEDOM 26

SELECTED BIBLIOGRAPHY ... 30
GLOSSARY 31
INTERNET SITES 32
INDEX 32

A NOTE ABOUT PRIMARY SOURCES

Primary sources are newspaper articles, photographs, speeches, or other documents that were created during an event. They are great ways to see how people spoke and felt during that time. You'll find primary sources from the time of slavery in the United States throughout this book. Within the text, primary source quotations are colored *red* and set in italic type.

COLONIAL SLAVE TRADE

*"... the slaves in the night were often heard making a howling ... kind of noise, something expressive of extreme **anguish**. I found that it was occasioned by finding themselves in a slave room, after dreaming that they had been ... amongst friends ..."*

—Thomas Trotter, a surgeon on a slave ship

Riding below deck, in the waves of the Atlantic, **enslaved** Africans experienced the nightmare that was a slave ship. The people on board had been kidnapped from their homes in Africa. They were chained together and forced into the dark underbelly of a ship. As many as 700 people rode below deck, not knowing where they were being taken. The air smelled of waste and vomit. Many cried out in fear.

This illustration appeared in *Harper's Weekly* magazine on June 2, 1860. It depicts Africans on the slave ship *Wildfire*.

anguish—extreme pain or fear
enslave—to make someone a slave

African people who were forced onto slave ships in the 1600s faced unthinkable conditions. But it was nothing compared to the life of slavery that awaited the prisoners in America. Slavery in America was a booming business for more than 200 years. When the ships docked, auctioneers sold the prisoners as slaves to the highest bidder. Many people felt slaves were necessary to build the economy. But many other people came to believe that slavery was wrong and should be stopped.

TRIANGULAR TRADE

Slavery had existed in Europe long before colonists settled in America. Europeans thought Africans lived uncivilized lives. And many believed black people were only good for labor.

As the British established colonies in North America, they needed laborers to develop the rough land. So they began bringing black people as slaves to America. When the slave ship *Desire* left from Massachusetts in 1636, the slave trade had begun.

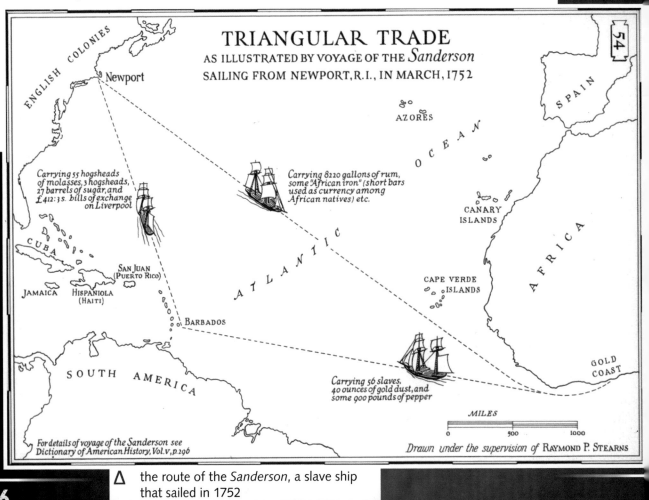

TRIANGULAR TRADE
AS ILLUSTRATED BY VOYAGE OF THE *Sanderson*
SAILING FROM NEWPORT, R.I., IN MARCH, 1752

ENGLISH COLONIES

Newport

AZORES

OCEAN

SPAIN

Carrying 55 hogsheads of molasses, 3 hogsheads, 27 barrels of sugar, and £412:3 s. bills of exchange on Liverpool

Carrying 8220 gallons of rum, some "African iron" (short bars used as currency among African natives) etc.

CANARY ISLANDS

CUBA

SAN JUAN (PUERTO RICO)

JAMAICA   HISPANIOLA (HAITI)

CAPE VERDE ISLANDS

AFRICA

ATLANTIC

BARBADOS

SOUTH AMERICA

Carrying 56 slaves, 40 ounces of gold dust, and some 900 pounds of pepper

GOLD COAST

MILES
0   500   1000

For details of voyage of the Sanderson see Dictionary of American History, Vol. v, p.296

Drawn under the supervision of RAYMOND P. STEARNS

△ the route of the *Sanderson*, a slave ship that sailed in 1752

Not all white colonists believed in slavery. A religious group called the Quakers passed the first antislavery resolution in 1688. It was the first American document that argued everyone should be equal.

The slave trade in America became a profitable business. *"The African Trade is a Trade of the [most] Advantage to this Kingdom of any we drive, and as it were all Profit ..."* claimed British merchant John Cary in 1745. Over time a system of **exporting** goods and **importing** enslaved people developed. Ships sailed from America to Africa with products such as rum. In Africa ship captains traded goods for men and women who had been kidnapped or captured during war. The ships would then sail to the Caribbean and South America. There they traded some of the slaves for molasses. Finally, the ships brought molasses and the rest of the slaves back to North America.

export—to send and sell goods to other countries
import—to bring goods into one country from another

SLAVERY IN A NEW NATION

For more than 100 years, the slave trade in America grew. The fertile land of the South needed many hands to tend its crops. By 1790 about 600,000 black people lived as slaves in the South. A few Northern white colonists began to speak out against slavery. But their concern was overshadowed by another issue.

The Revolutionary War (1775–1783) changed the colonies forever. American colonists, angry with British rule, fought for their independence. Some slaves joined the colonists in the fight, hoping they would be given freedom. At the Battle of Bunker Hill in June 1775, enslaved black soldier Salem Poor fought bravely. Fourteen officers signed a petition saying he *"... behaved liked an experienced officer, as well as an excellent soldier ... In the person of this said negro, centers a brave and gallant soldier."*

The British hoped to weaken the Americans' fight, so they promised freedom to slaves who joined their side. British commander in chief Sir Henry Clinton wrote the Philipsburg Proclamation. In it he said, *"... I do promise to every Negroe who shall desert the Rebel Standard, full security ..."* Many slaves joined the British.

Peter Salem, far left, was another slave who fought for the colonies during the Revolutionary War. Salem was given his freedom in exchange for joining the Continental army.

Clinton's 1779 Philipsburg Proclamation

A CONSTITUTIONAL COMPROMISE

By 1783 the Americans had won the war and were free of Britain's rule. Victory did not, however, mean freedom for everyone in the newly formed United States.

Many Northern citizens objected to slavery and wanted it **abolished** in the new country. New York lawmaker John Jay wrote, *"The honour of the States, as well as justice and humanity ... loudly call upon them to **emancipate** these unhappy people."* But many, especially in the South, depended on slavery. Connecticut lawmaker Oliver Ellsworth felt the new Constitution should not address slavery. *"Let us not intermeddle. As population increases; poor laborers will be so plenty as to render slaves useless."*

Leaders debated the rules that would make up the new Constitution. They decided each state would choose to allow slavery or not. Leaders also agreed the number of lawmakers each state had in the House of Representatives would be based on population. The more people in the state, the more representatives the state would have. But what about slaves?

abolish—to put an end to something officially
emancipate—to free from the control of another

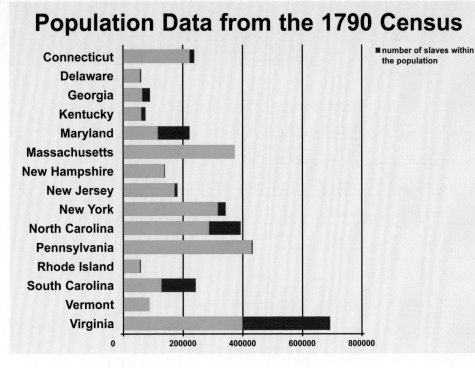

Population Data from the 1790 Census

Legend: ■ number of slaves within the population

States (top to bottom): Connecticut, Delaware, Georgia, Kentucky, Maryland, Massachusetts, New Hampshire, New Jersey, New York, North Carolina, Pennsylvania, Rhode Island, South Carolina, Vermont, Virginia

X-axis: 0, 200000, 400000, 600000, 800000

Southern leaders wanted to count each slave as one person. But Northerners knew this would give the South more lawmakers—and more power. The North and South compromised by counting each slave as three-fifths of a person. It also said Congress could not end the slave trade until 1808. These compromises did not satisfy anyone, and more arguments over slavery were to come.

◁ Many enslaved people were forced to work in cotton fields, as shown in this undated photograph.

CRITICAL THINKING

Review the population data taken from the 1790 census. Use the data to explain why Northerners did not want to count each slave as one person.

LIFE AS A SLAVE

"Master he be a hard hard man.
Hoe Emma Hoe, Hoe Emma Hoe.
Sell my people away from me.
Hoe Emma Hoe, Hoe Emma Hoe."

—"Hoe Emma Hoe," a slave work song

By the early 1800s, most northern states had outlawed slavery. But southern states grew more and more dependent on slave labor to farm the huge plantations.

Slave owners bought and sold slaves at auctions. Black people could only watch as their families were broken up. They saw their husbands, wives, and children sold to faraway owners. In most cases families were never reunited.

Posters, like this one from Spring Hill, Arkansas, advertised upcoming auctions and the slaves that would be sold. ▷

NEGROES FOR SALE.

☞ Will be sold at public auction, at Spring Hill, in the County of Hempstead, on a credit of twelve months, on Friday the 28th day of this present month, 15 young and valuable Slaves, consisting of 9 superior Men & Boys, between 12 and 27 years of age, one woman about 43 years who is a good washer and cook, one woman about twenty-seven, and one very likely young woman with three children.

Also at the same time, and on the same terms, three Mules, about forty head of Cattle, plantation tools, one waggon, and a first rate Gin stand, manufactured by Pratt &Co.

Bond with two or more approved securities will be required. Sale to commence at 10 o'clock.

E. E. Hundley,
W. Robinson,
H. M. Robinson.

Spring Hill, Jan. 6th, 1842.

▲ Artists created pictures of the whippings slaves received based on eyewitness accounts.

No laws controlled how owners treated the slaves on their plantations. Some masters were kind. But many more were cruel. Years after she was freed, former slave Ella Wilson recalled, *"My [master] used to throw me in a buck and whip me. He would put my hands together and tie them ... He would whip me on one side till that was sore and full of blood and then he would whip me on the other side till that was all tore up."*

DEFENDING SLAVERY

Some Americans believed the slavery system not only helped masters, but it helped slaves too. In 1854 Nehemiah Adams published *A South-Side View of Slavery*. Adams was against slavery until he took a trip to the South. He claimed he saw only happy slaves during his visit. He wrote of one woman, *"She says that if she were to buy her freedom, she would have no one to take care of her for the rest of her life. Now her master is responsible for her support. She has no care about the future. Old age, sickness, poverty, do not trouble her."*

▽ the title page of Adams' book

A

SOUTH-SIDE VIEW OF

SLAVERY;

OR,

THREE MONTHS AT THE SOUTH,

IN 1854.

BY

NEHEMIAH ADAMS, D. D.

THIRD EDITION.

RICHMOND, VA.:
PUBLISHED BY A. MORRIS.
1855.

Slave owners worried that slaves would run away. In order to prevent escapes, Southern lawmakers pushed through the Fugitive Slave Law of 1850. The law said escaped slaves had to be returned to their masters and that anyone who helped them could be punished.

In 1835 George McDuffie, governor of South Carolina, gave a speech to the South Carolina legislature. He spoke of the popular belief among southern whites that blacks were not as smart as whites. *"They have all the qualities that fit them for slaves, and not one of those that would fit them to be freemen. They are utterly unqualified not only for rational freedom, but for self-government of any kind."* McDuffie declared, *"Emancipation would be a positive curse, depriving them of a guardianship essential to their happiness ..."*

CRITICAL THINKING

McDuffie claimed that freeing slaves would take away the key to their happiness. Compare his

THE LIBERATOR. WM. LLOYD GARRISON, Editor. Our Country is the World, our Countrymen are all Mankind. J. B. YERRINTON & SON, Printer. VOL. XXVII. NO. 43. BOSTON, FRIDAY, OCTOBER 23, 1857. WHOLE NUMBER, 1398.

FIGHTING SLAVERY

"Our Country is the World, our Countrymen are all Mankind." This phrase was the motto of *The Liberator*, an antislavery newspaper. The motto rang true for all **abolitionists** too.

The abolitionist movement started as a whisper and grew to a roar. Free African-Americans and white people united to end slavery in the United States. William Lloyd Garrison, publisher of *The Liberator* and famous abolitionist, spoke of what was at the very heart of their fight, saying, *"... every sixth man, woman, child and babe in the United States is a slave, one who has no more rights than a beast ..."*

16

abolitionist—a person who worked to end slavery

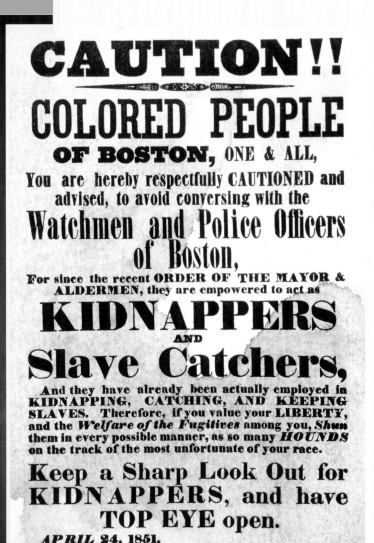

CAUTION!!
COLORED PEOPLE
OF BOSTON, ONE & ALL,

You are hereby respectfully CAUTIONED and advised, to avoid conversing with the

Watchmen and Police Officers of Boston,

For since the recent ORDER OF THE MAYOR & ALDERMEN, they are empowered to act as

KIDNAPPERS
AND
Slave Catchers,

And they have already been actually employed in KIDNAPPING, CATCHING, AND KEEPING SLAVES. Therefore, if you value your LIBERTY, and the *Welfare of the Fugitives* among you, *Shun* them in every possible manner, as so many *HOUNDS* on the track of the most unfortunate of your race.

Keep a Sharp Look Out for KIDNAPPERS, and have TOP EYE open.

APRIL 24, 1851.

△ This pamphlet, from April 24, 1851, warned African-Americans in Boston to be on the lookout for police who were trying to catch them and sell them back into slavery.

Escaped slaves lent their voices to the abolitionist movement too. Speaking publicly against slavery was a great risk to their safety. But many, like Frederick Douglass, used their personal stories to convince others to join the fight. In his autobiography, printed in 1845, Douglass described the violence one slave experienced at the hands of a cruel master. *"Before he commenced whipping Aunt Hester, he took her into the kitchen ... He made her get upon the stool, and tied her hands to the hook ... Her arms were stretched up at their full length, so that she stood upon the ends of her toes ... and after rolling up his sleeves, he commenced to lay on the heavy cowskin ..."*

THE UNDERGROUND RAILROAD

Many abolitionists found a secret way to fight slavery. The Underground Railroad was a system of hiding places that led slaves to freedom in the North.

Abolitionist Martha C. Wright described the journey on the Underground Railroad in a letter.

"... They walked all night, carrying the little ones, and spread the old comfort[er] on the frozen ground, in some dense thicket where they all hid, while Harriet went out foraging, and sometimes [could] not get back till dark, fearing she [would] be followed. Then, if they had crept further in, and she couldn't find them, she [would] whistle, or sing certain hymns and they would answer."

Few photos exist of the Underground Railroad because it was conducted in secret. Artists re-created scenes like this one showing Harriet Tubman helping slaves escape.

The "Harriet" that Wright mentioned was escaped slave Harriet Tubman, one of the Underground Railroad's best known conductors. Conductors risked their lives to lead slaves to free northern states.

Slave owners felt that slaves were their property. They offered rewards for escaped slaves. If caught, slaves were sent back to their masters and were harshly punished. Anyone caught helping them were considered slave stealers. Slave stealers could be fined, jailed, or killed.

ROUTES OF THE UNDERGROUND RAILROAD

It is estimated that Harriet Tubman helped 300 people find freedom.

The issue of slavery deeply divided people in the United States. And it deeply divided the federal government too. That division became very clear when Missouri wanted to join the Union as a slave state.

Missouri applied for statehood in 1818. At that time the country had an equal number of free states and slave states. Adding Missouri threatened to upset that balance. Lawmakers argued for years over what to do. Congressman Arthur Livermore of New Hampshire wondered, *"How long will the desire of wealth render us blind to the sin of holding ... our fellow men in chains!"* Tempers flared, and Southern lawmakers began threatening to leave the Union. Representative Thomas Cobb of Georgia warned if slavery were limited or abolished *"... the Union will be dissolved."*

In 1820 Maine applied for statehood and made a compromise possible. Speaker of the House Henry Clay argued that Maine and Missouri should be admitted together. Maine would be a free state, and Missouri would allow slaves. The solution seemed simple, but too much anger boiled on both sides. After weeks of debate, Senators agreed to admit both states. They also decided where slavery would be allowed going forward. They agreed that slavery would not be allowed in areas north of Missouri's southern border.

The Missouri Compromise was just a bandage on a huge wound. Former President Thomas Jefferson wrote that he feared the compromise would be the end of the Union. He wrote that the compromise *"... like a fire bell in the night, awakened and filled me with terror. I considered it at once as the **knell** of the Union."* Jefferson realized that a line drawn on a map could not settle an issue as large as slavery.

△ the committee report that includes the Missouri Compromise, dated March 1, 1820

THE MISSOURI COMPROMISE

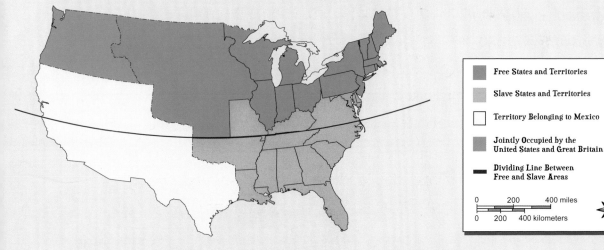

▨	Free States and Territories
▨	Slave States and Territories
☐	Territory Belonging to Mexico
▨	Jointly Occupied by the United States and Great Britain
▬	Dividing Line Between Free and Slave Areas

0   200   400 miles

0   200   400 kilometers

N

knell—a sound of a bell, especially when rung slowly as for a death, funeral, or disaster

TENSION TURNS TO VIOLENCE

Tensions over slavery continued to grow between the North and South. Abolitionists pushed hard for an immediate end to slavery. Slave owners pushed for laws that kept their way of life in place.

As divisions grew deeper, violent slave rebellions erupted. The most famous was Nat Turner's rebellion in August 1831. Turner was a slave in Virginia. He and about 70 other slaves tried to free themselves by killing almost 60 white people, including Turner's owners. In *The Confessions of Nat Turner*, Turner confessed that God had told him to rebel. *"... the Spirit instantly appeared to me and said the Serpent [devil] was loosened ... and that I should take it on and fight against the Serpent ..."*

HORRID MASSACRE IN VIRGINIA.

▷ Created shortly after Turner's rebellion in 1831, an artist created this woodcut of what the scene might have looked like.

Charlestown, Va, 2ͩ December, 1859.
I John Brown am now quite certain that the crimes of this guilty, land: will never be purged away; but with Blood: I had as I now think: vainly flattered myself that without very much bloodshed; it might be done.

△ John Brown was an abolitionist who believed violence was the only way to end slavery. He planned to steal weapons and give them to slaves, but soldiers stopped him. Before he was hanged for treason, Brown wrote this note on December 2, 1859. Many believe the note predicted the U.S. Civil War.

In revenge, angry whites killed about 100 innocent slaves. The *Richmond Enquirer*, on August 30, 1831, described the white community's feelings about Turner and his followers. *"What strikes us as the most remarkable thing ... is the horrible ferocity of these monsters."*

In 1854 the Kansas-Nebraska Act undid the work of the Missouri Compromise. Lawmakers decided that residents should decide if slavery would be allowed in a new state. To keep slavery out of the new state of Kansas, abolitionists moved there by the hundreds. Proslavery Missourians encouraged raids on these settlers. Hundreds of people were wounded or killed in "Bleeding Kansas."

The violence did nothing to settle the issues. In fact it only made the situation worse.

WAR

In December 1860 Jefferson's fear that the Union would collapse began to come true. South Carolina decided to **secede**. By May 1861, 10 more Southern states had left. The states withdrew from the Union because they feared the new president, Abraham Lincoln, would take away states' rights, including slavery. Before taking office Lincoln had said, *"'A house divided against itself cannot stand.' I believe this Government cannot endure, permanently, half slave and half free."*

In April 1861 shots were fired at Fort Sumter in South Carolina. The Civil War had begun. The next four years were a blur of bloody battles. Roughly 2 percent of the population was killed. The weight of war weighed heavily upon Lincoln's shoulders.

▷ This image, called "Reading the Emancipation Proclamation," was created around 1864 and was included with a pamphlet about Lincoln's action.

secede—to formally withdraw from a group or an organization

the Emancipation Proclamation from 1863

Lincoln wrote, *"My paramount object in this struggle is to save the Union, and is not either to save or destroy Slavery. If I could save the Union without freeing any slave, I would do it, and if I could save it by freeing all the slaves, I would do it, and if I could do it by freeing some and leaving others alone, I would also do that."*

About two years into the war, Lincoln issued the Emancipation Proclamation. This order stated that, *"... all persons held as slaves within any State ... shall be then, thenceforward, and forever free ..."* This order granted freedom to enslaved people in the seceded states.

Jefferson Davis, president of the seceded states, responded to Lincoln in July 1864. *"We are fighting for INDEPENDENCE ... You may 'emancipate' every negro in the Confederacy, but we will be free. We will govern ourselves ..."*

CRITICAL THINKING

Compare Lincoln's quotation from before taking office with what he said after the war began. How did becoming president change how Lincoln spoke about slavery in the United States?

Many people in the North and South celebrated Lincoln's proclamation. Colonel Thomas Wentworth Higginson remembered the celebration in Port Royal, South Carolina. *"... the President's Proclamation was read ... Then followed an incident so simple, so touching ... The very moment the speaker had ceased, and just as I ... waved the flag, which now for the first time meant anything to these poor people, there suddenly arose ... singing ... 'My Country, 'tis of thee, Sweet land of liberty, Of thee I sing!'"*

The Emancipation Proclamation was signed on January 1, 1863, but the Civil War was nowhere near its end. It would take a series of defeats and a shortage of supplies for the **Confederates** to accept defeat. By the spring of 1865, all the major Confederate armies surrendered. When the Union cavalry captured Confederate President Jefferson Davis on May 10, 1865, the Confederates knew the fight was over.

Printed in Frank Leslie's illustrated newspaper on January 24, 1863, "Emancipation Day in South Carolina" depicts the joyous scene Colonel Higginson described. ▷

Confederate—a person who supported the cause of the southern states during the Civil War

After the war the Southern states rejoined the Union. Many white Southerners were not happy with their new lives. Eva Jones from Georgia wrote in June 1865, *"I suppose you have learned even in the more secluded portions of the country that slavery is entirely abolished ... I know it is only intended for a greater humiliation and loss to us ..."*

But former slaves, like Mary Prince, rejoiced. Prince said, *"All slaves want to be free—to be free is very sweet ... I have been a slave myself—I know what slaves feel—I can tell by myself what other slaves feel, and by what they have told me. The man that says slaves be quite happy in slavery—that they don't want to be free—that man is either ignorant or a lying person."*

MAKING IT LAW

*"Neither slavery nor involuntary servitude, except
as a punishment for crime ... shall exist within the
United States ..."*   —13th Amendment

The U.S. Constitution is the law of the land. In
January 1865 Congress passed a change to that ruling
document—the 13th Amendment. This change would make
slavery illegal in the United States. But in order to make
the change official, 27 of the 36 states in the Union had to
ratify it. Most Northern states approved the change quickly.
But Southern states, still angry and rebuilding from the war,
were resistant. Finally, in December 1865 enough states had
ratified the amendment. Slavery was officially and forever
banned from the country.

But that didn't mean life was instantly better for
African-Americans. Freedman Houston Hartsfield Holloway
wrote, *"For we colored people did not know how to be
free and the white people did not know how to have a
free colored person about them."* Congress began an
era of Reconstruction that lasted from 1866 to 1877.
Reconstruction helped blacks and whites learn to live
together. Formerly enslaved people began voting, buying
land, seeking jobs, going to school, and using public spaces.

ratify—to formally approve

This new way of life was a difficult adjustment for black and white people. Many Southern whites, still bitter about the outcome of the war, refused to treat black citizens equally. But African-Americans celebrated their new freedoms.

"Now dat's de way we keeps de 'casion, Happy bright and free,
And we bless good [Master] Lincoln, [Wherever] we may be.
De colored troops fought nobly, dat's what all de papers say.
And now dey march to vict'ry on Emancipation day."
—"Emancipation Day"
by G.L. Stout and Dave Braham, 1876

◁ 13th Amendment to the U.S. Constitution from 1865

SELECTED BIBLIOGRAPHY

Adams, Nehemiah. *A South-Side View of Slavery.* Online by The Johns Hopkins University Sheridan Libraries. https://archive.org/details/southsideviewofsl00adam

"A Letter from President Lincoln.; Reply to Horace Greeley. Slavery and the Union The Restoration of the Union the Paramount Object." August 22, 1862. Online by *The New York Times.* http://www.nytimes.com/1862/08/24/news/letter-president-lincoln-reply-horace-greeley-slavery-union-restoration-union.html

Douglass, Frederick. *Narrative of the Life of Frederick Douglass: An American Slave.* Online by Project Gutenberg. http://www.gutenberg.org/files/23/23-h/23-h.htm

Garrison, William Lloyd. "American Slavery: Address on the Subject of American Slavery, and the Progress of the Cause of Freedom Throughout the World." September 2, 1846. Online by the Samuel J. May Anti-Slavery Collection at Cornell University. http://ebooks.library.cornell.edu/cgi/t/text/pageviewer-idx?c=mayantislavery;cc=mayantislavery;rgn=full%20text;idno=10841913;didno=10841913;view=image;seq=1;node=10841913%3A1

Livermore, Arthur. "Address to House of Representatives." Annals of Congress, House of Representatives, 15th Congress, 2nd Session. Pages 1191 & 1192 of 1216. Online by American Memory at the Library of Congress. http://memory.loc.gov/cgi-bin/ampage?collId=llac&fileName=033/llac033.db&recNum=593

Stout, G.L., and David Braham. "Emancipation Day: Song and Chorus." New York: Wm. A. Pond & Co, 1876. Online by Brown University Library Center for Digital Scholarship. http://library.brown.edu/cds/catalog/catalog.php?verb=render&id=1073506640187500&colid=3

Wilson, Ella. "Interview with Wilson, Ella." WPA Slave Narrative Project, Arkansas Narratives, Volume 2, Part 7. Online by the Federal Writers Project, United States Works Projects Administration; Manuscript Division, Library of Congress. http://memory.loc.gov/cgi-bin/query/S?ammem/mesnbib:@field(AUTHOR+@od1(Wilson,+Ella))

GLOSSARY

abolish (uh-BOL-ish)—to put an end to something officially

abolitionist (ab-uh-LI-shuhn-ist)—a person who worked to end slavery

anguish (AYN-guish)—extreme pain or fear

Confederate (kuhn-FE-der-uht)—a person who supported the cause of the Southern states during the Civil War; the Southern states called themselves the Confederate States of America

emancipate (e-MAN-si-payt)—to free from control of another

enslave (in-SLAYV)—to make someone a slave

export (EK-sport)—to send and sell goods to other countries

import (IM-port)—to bring goods into one country from another

knell (NEL)—a sound of a bell, especially when rung slowly as for a death, funeral, or disaster

ratify (RAH-tuh-fy)—to formally approve

secede (si-SEED)—to formally withdraw from a group or an organization, often to form another organization

INTERNET SITES

FactHound offers a safe, fun way to find Internet sites related to this book. All of the sites on FactHound have been researched by our staff.

Here's all you do:

Visit *www.facthound.com*

Type in this code: 9781491418390

 Check out projects, games and lots more at
www.capstonekids.com

INDEX

abolitionists, 16–17, 18, 22, 23

Emancipation Proclamation, 25, 26

Kansas-Nebraska Act, 23

Missouri Compromise, 20–21, 23

Nat Turner's rebellion, 22–23

Philipsburg Proclamation, 8

Reconstruction, 28–29

slave auctions, 5, 12
slave ships, 4–5, 6–7

treatment of slaves, 4, 5, 12, 13, 17, 19
triangular trade, 6–7

Underground Railroad, 18–19
U.S. Civil War, 23, 24–25, 26–27
U.S. Constitution, 10–11, 28–29